Alphabet Puppets!

Plus Blends & Digraphs!

46 Fun Paper Bag Puppet Patterns!

Copyright © 2006
Teacher's Friend Publications,
A Scholastic Company
All rights reserved.
Printed in the U.S.A.

ISBN-13 978-0-439-89307-7
ISBN-10 0-439-89307-0

Cover design and all illustrations: Karen Sevaly
Graphic Layout: Susan Isaacs & Debbie Schultz

teacher's friend
publications

Teacher's Friend,
A Scholastic Company

Making the Most of This Book!

Teach and practice important phonemic awareness and emergent reading skills with the help of these simple puppet patterns!

In this book you will find a pattern to make paperbag puppets for each letter of the alphabet in addition to several blends and digraphs. Young children love making these creative, cute puppets and learning each letter's distinctive sound. With the use of puppets, children will be motivated to practice phonemic skills both at school and home. Here are a few suggestions for making and using these puppet patterns:

Making the Puppets - All of the patterns are reproducible. Simply copy the patterns on to art paper or colored construction paper. Cut along the heavy lines. The children can color, cut, and glue the patterns to small paper lunch bags to make each puppet. Glue the upper part of the pattern to the bottom flap of the paper bag. Then lift the flap and glue the lower part of the pattern to the bag. Encourage the children to embellish their puppets by adding glitter, sequins, etc.

Letter of the Week - Introduce each letter (or blend or digraph) by designating the specific letter as "Letter of the Week!" Have each child make his or her own "letter" puppet. Children can use their puppets to orally participate during phonics or reading lessons. After each letter, blend, or digraph has been mastered, the puppet can be taken home as an award and shared with family members.

Reinforcement and Practice - Encourage the students to find the specific letter, blend, or digraph wherever they can in their environment. Point out the initial letter sound words in reading books, charts, labels, etc. List these words on your class word wall.

Other Ways to Use the Puppets - Many of the puppets can be used in a variety of other ways. Try these ideas:
- Teach about specific animals using the animal puppets.
    Mammals: *bear, cat, elephant, goat, hippo, kangaroo, lion, monkey, pig, raccoon, whale*
    Birds: *duck, chicken*
    Ocean Animals: *crab, fish, octopus, whale*
    Reptiles and Amphibians: *frog, snake,* and *turtle*
- Teach about the weather using the *sun* and *umbrella* puppets.
- Teach about nutrition using the *apple, ice cream, nut,* and *grapes* puppets.
- Encourage students to create simple plays and skits that can be acted out using the paperbag puppets.

Aa

Apple
Puppet

Bb

Bear Puppet

Cc

Cat
Puppet

Dd

Duck
Puppet

Ee

Elephant
Puppet

7

Gg

Goat
Puppet

Hh

Hippo
Puppet

Alphabet Puppets! Plus Blends and Digraphs!

Ii

Ice
Cream
Puppet

Jj

Joker Puppet

Alphabet Puppets! Plus Blends and Digraphs!

Kangaroo
Puppet

continued on page 14

Kk

Kangaroo
Puppet

continued from page 13

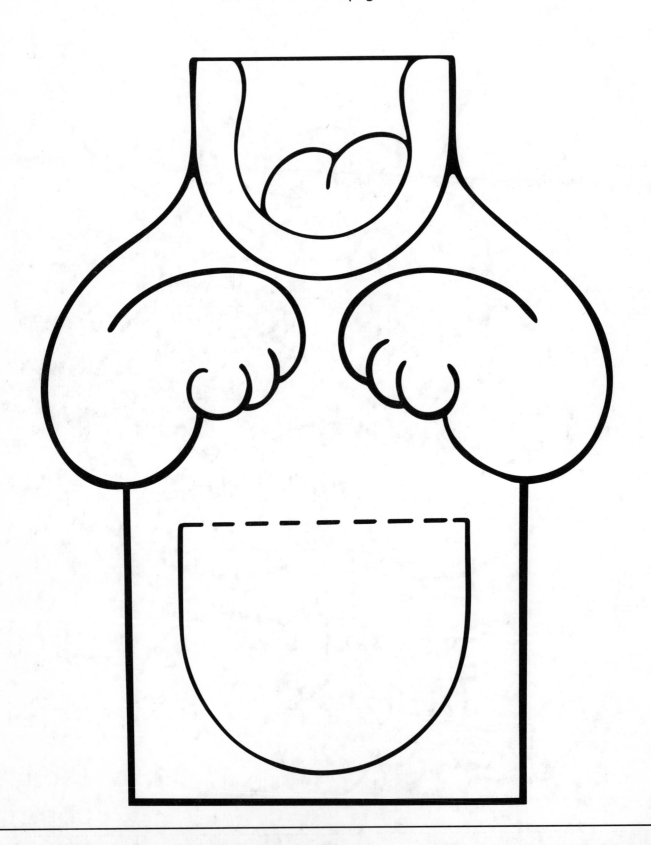

Lion
Puppet

Nut
Puppet

Oo

Pig
Puppet

Qq

Queen
Puppet

Raccoon
Puppet

Ss

Turtle
Puppet

Tt

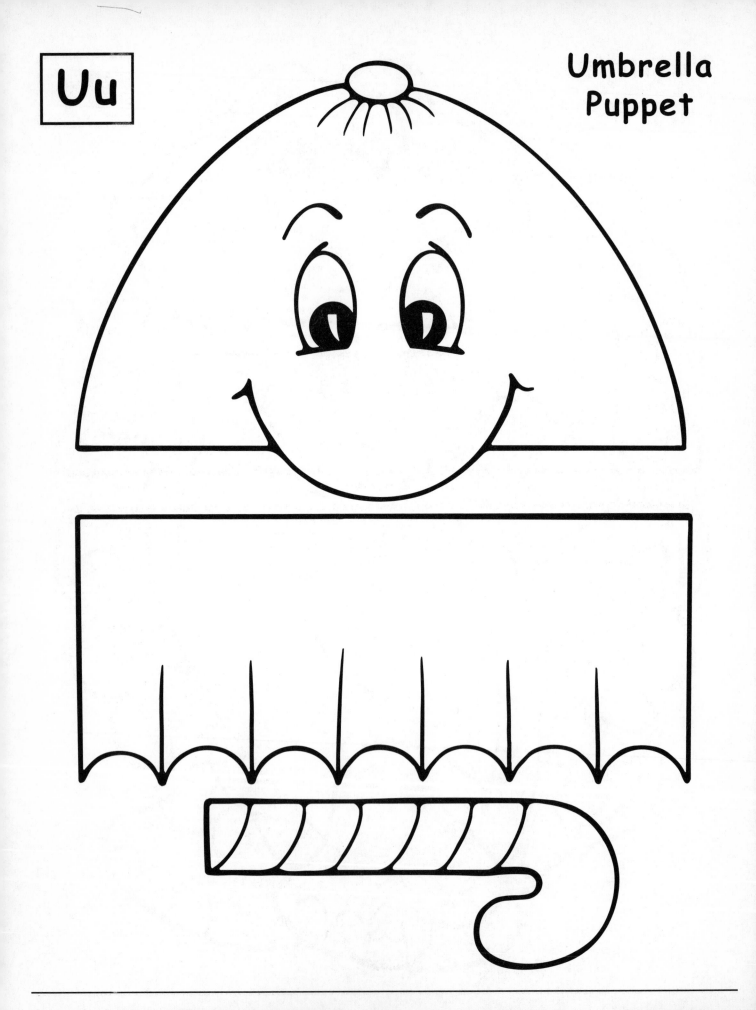

Uu

Valentine
Puppet

Ww

Worm
Puppet

Alphabet Puppets! Plus Blends and Digraphs!

Xylophone
Puppet

Yy

Yarn
Puppet

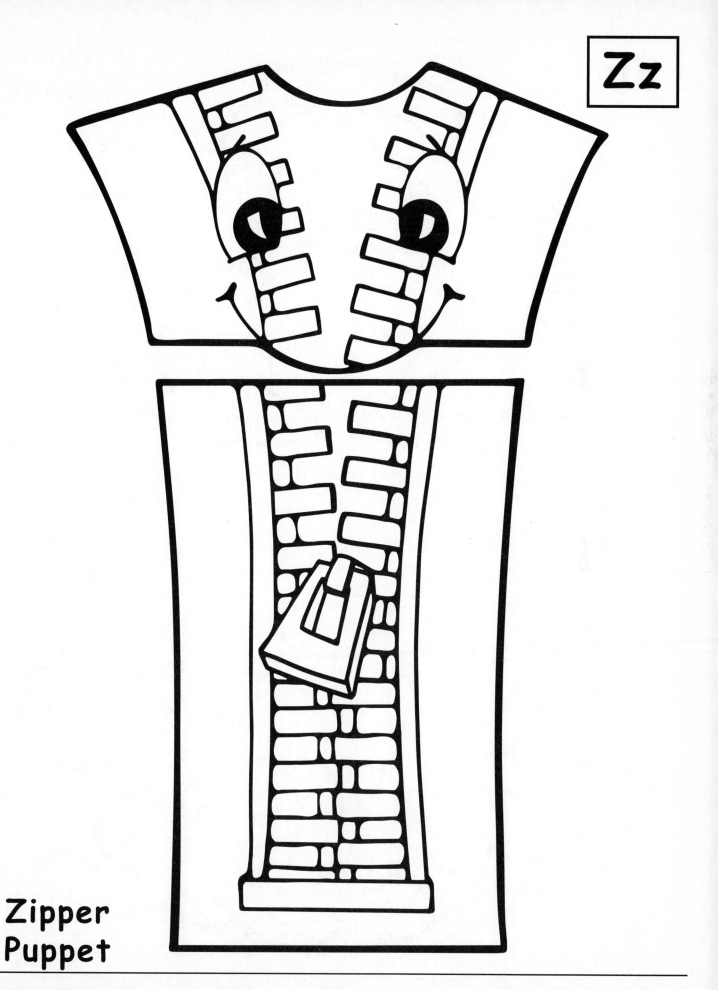

Zipper
Puppet

ch

Clock
Puppet

cl

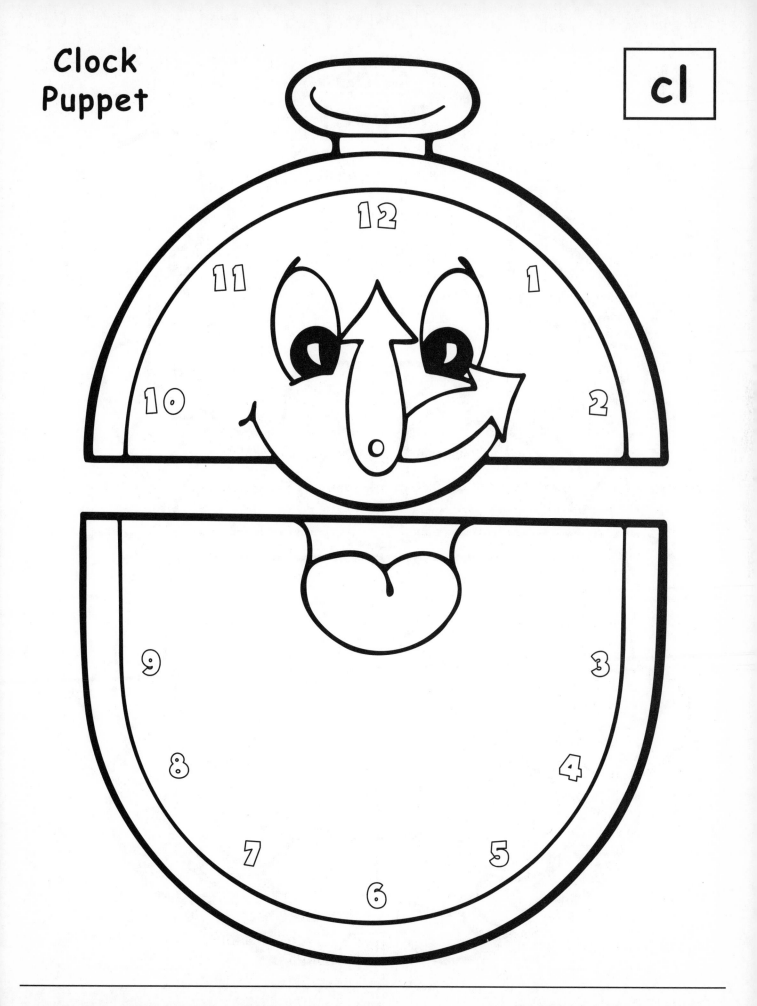

Crab
Puppet

Drum
Puppet

dr

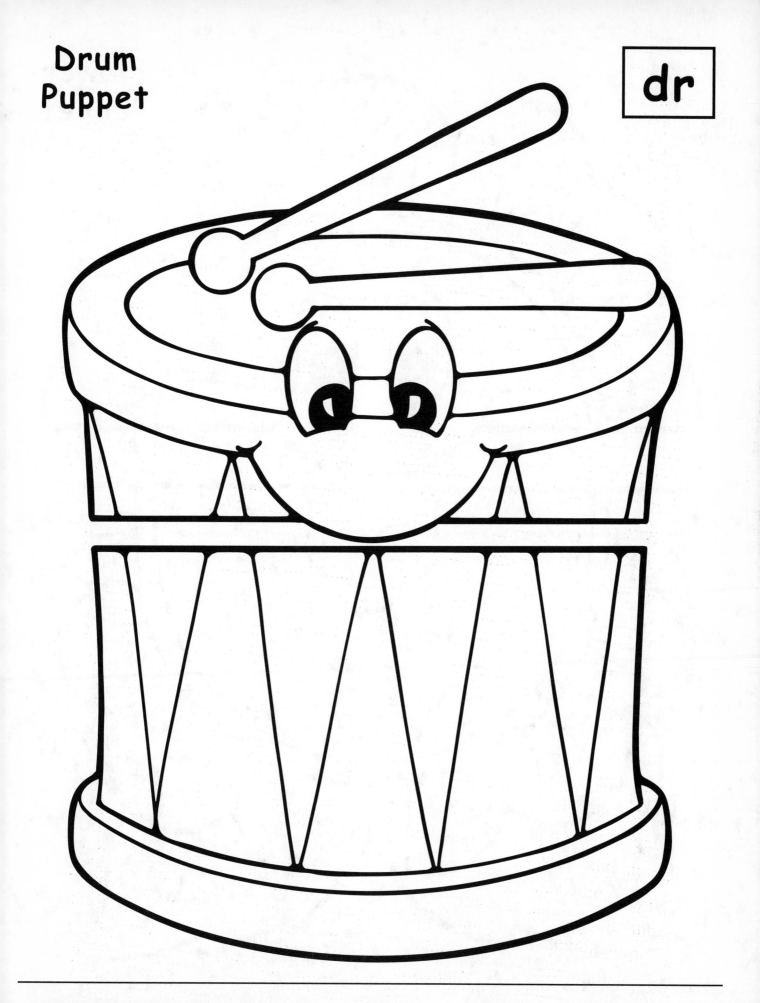

fl

Flower
Puppet

Frog
Puppet

fr

gl

Glue
Puppet

GLUE

Grapes
Puppet

pl

Plant
Puppet

Present
Puppet

pr

sh

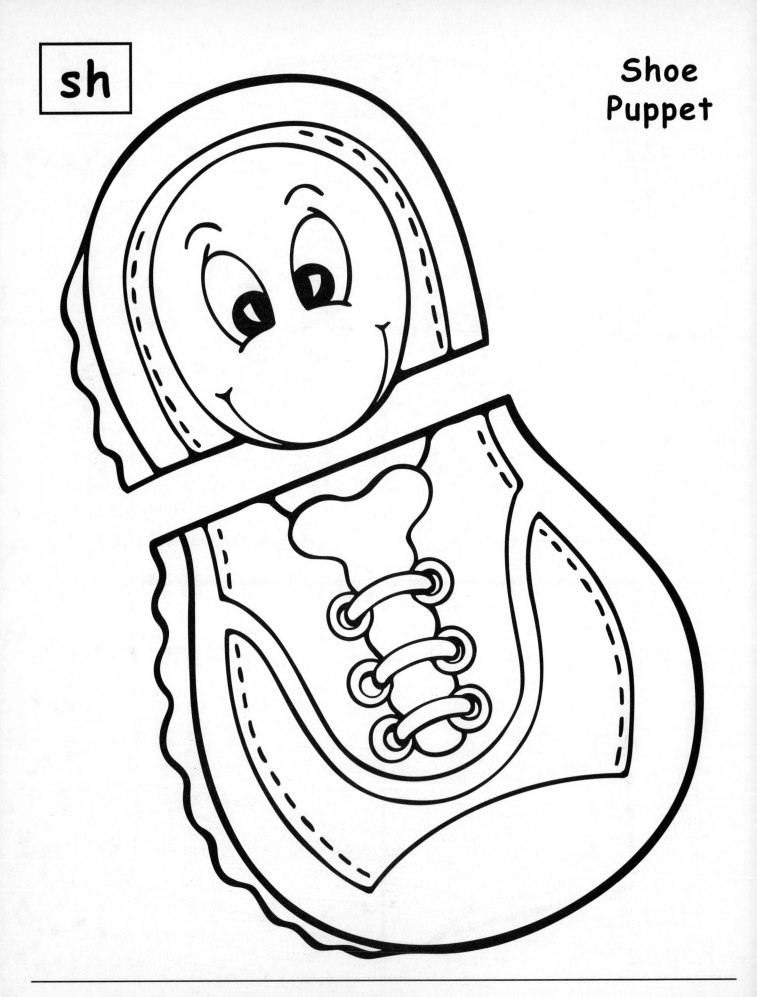

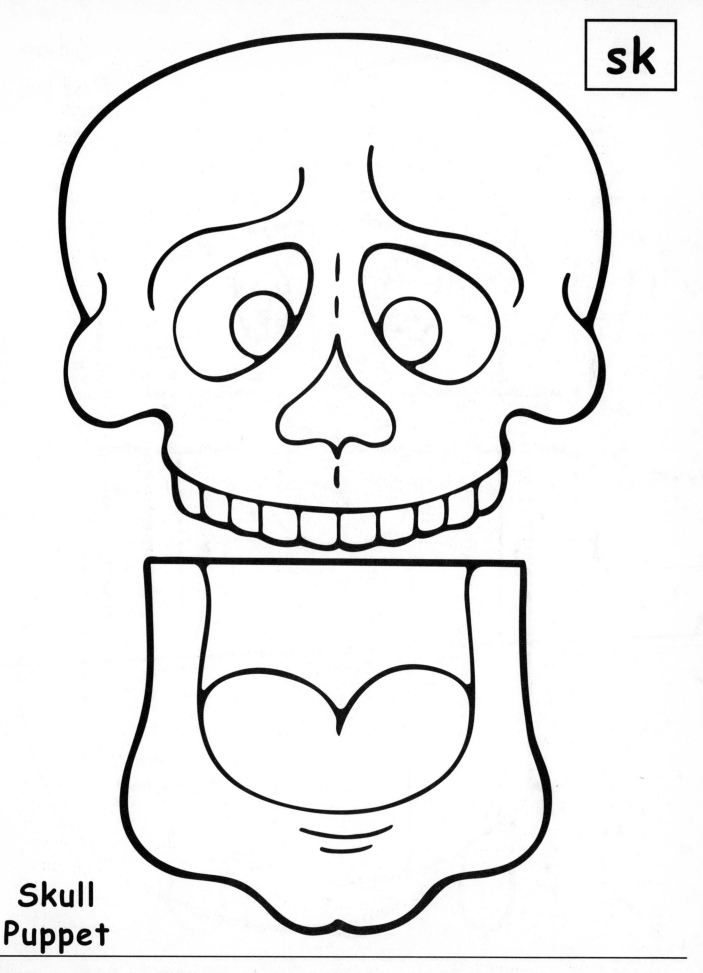

sk

Skull
Puppet

sl

sn

Snake
Puppet

43 Alphabet Puppets! Plus Blends and Digraphs!

sp

Stocking
Puppet

tr

Whale
Puppet

wh

Happy
Face
Puppet